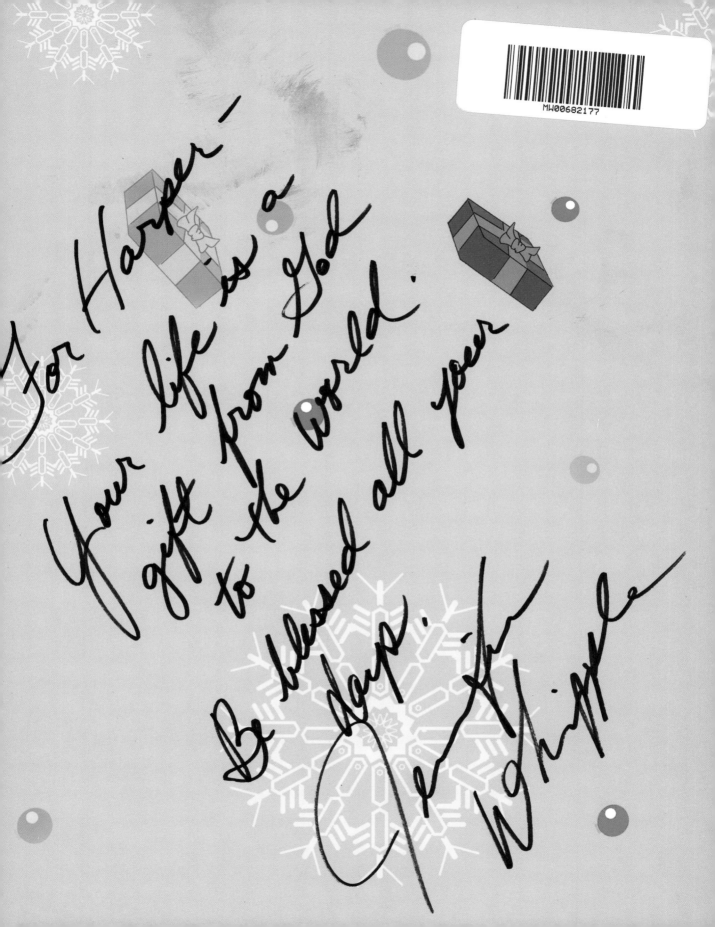

For Harper -
Your life is a
gift from God
to the World.

Be blessed all your
days.

W Shipp

Christmas
on a
Spoon

By
Jennifer Whipple

Illustrated by
John C. Jorif II

ZOË LIFE
PUBLISHING

Published by:
Zoë Life Publishing
P.O. Box 871066
Canton, MI 48187 USA
www.zoelifepub.com

Author: Jennifer Whipple
Illustrator: John Jorif
Editorial Team: Pam Gossiaux and Jessica Colvin

First U.S. Edition 2009

Publisher's Cataloging-In-Publication Data

Whipple, Jennifer.
    Christmas on a spoon / Jennifer Whipple. — 1st ed.
p. cm.
    ISBN-13: 978-1-934363-07-2
    ISBN-10: 1934363073

1. Jesus Christ. 2. Christmas. 3. Christian Theology. 4. Family—Christian Life.
    I. Jorif III, John C., ill. II. Title
BT315.W6 2009
230—dc22   2009927356

Summary: A delightful tale of a family, trying to hide their disappointment as they go through the rituals of Christmas day. Grandfather arrives and brightens the day. As he tells a story of a discarded silver spoon found in a trash heap, given as a gift, they are reminded the reason for the season is Jesus, that Christmas is not about the gifts or even the grand feast, but that Christmas means, what Christmas means, despite our silver spoons.

For current information about releases by Jennifer Whipple or other releases from Zoë Life Publishing, visit our website: http://www.zoelifepub.com

Printed in the United States of America

v6.6 05 15 09

Dedication

For Jesus. Thanks for everything.

Acknowledgments

A huge thanks to my husband, Rick, and our girls for their support and understanding even when the going was tough. I love you all so very much.

Thank you to my mom, my siblings and their families, and my husband's family. Your enthusiastic support inspired me to reach higher.

A big shout of thanks up to heaven to my dad who always believed in me in every way.

To Sabrina and Brian Adams and their wonderful Zoë Life team: Thank you for giving me a chance and teaching me along the way.

Much gratitude to my neighbors, the Reames family: Cathy who read my story back to me aloud and Tammy who cried when I got it right.

My most sincere appreciation to my Bethesda Bible Church family, especially the Warner Cell Group, who prayerfully waged war in the heavenly places with me. Glory be to Jesus, the most powerful weapon ever known.

2

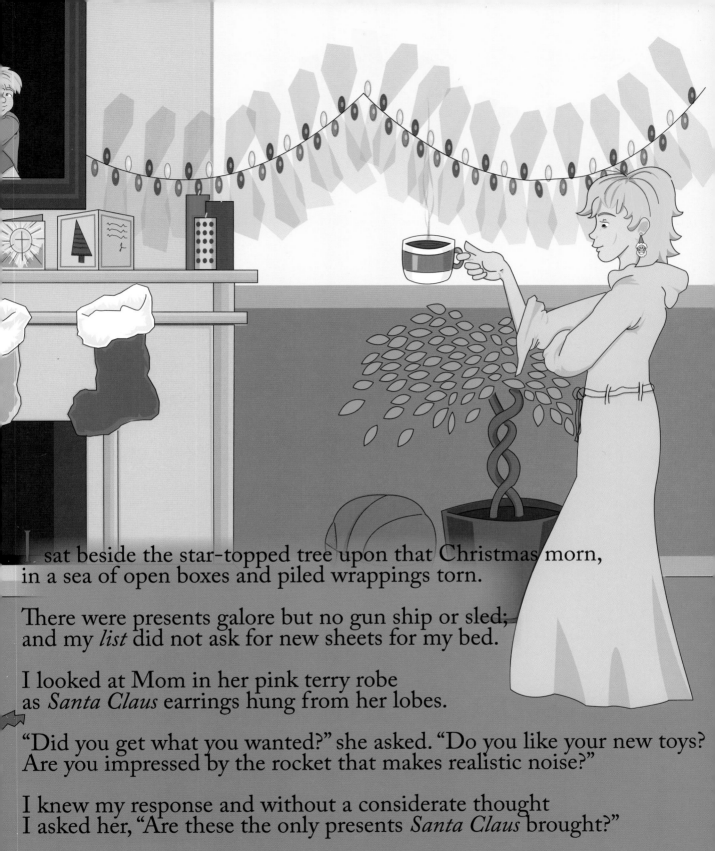

I sat beside the star-topped tree upon that Christmas morn,
in a sea of open boxes and piled wrappings torn.

There were presents galore but no gun ship or sled;
and my *list* did not ask for new sheets for my bed.

I looked at Mom in her pink terry robe
as *Santa Claus* earrings hung from her lobes.

"Did you get what you wanted?" she asked. "Do you like your new toys?
Are you impressed by the rocket that makes realistic noise?"

I knew my response and without a considerate thought
I asked her, "Are these the only presents *Santa Claus* brought?"

"I asked for a gun ship with a landing deck on the rear..."
Then Mom interrupted me and said, "Maybe next year."

3

I gathered up my things at Mom's command.
So far this Christmas had not gone as planned.

I had been a good boy and this didn't seem fair.
My head hung heavy as I climbed up the last stair.

5

Mom says that coffee tastes best on the first morning swallow, when her head is still cloudy and her stomach is hollow.

6   Mom placed her lips on the steaming edge of her mug and she murmured, "No *thank you*? Not even a hug?"

"You think I wanted the apron or cookbook?"
    she mumbled.
"Or the Santa that does the silly acrobat tumbles?"

"Now jewelry would make me float like a cloud,
but you don't hear me complaining aloud."

Oh, the resentment she felt had given her pause
to rethink her position on old *Santa Claus*.

Over her shoulder were loud clinks in the kitchen
where Dad was full of pep and ready to pitch in.

He placed the turkey in the oven with a smile,
and said to the turkey, "I'll baste you in a while."

8

Creative cooking was a hobby for Dad,
    and how it showed in the extra poundage he had!

    The fruit cut that morning was beginning to wilt,
        so he opened the doughnuts and pondered his guilt.

        He said to his belly, "Aw, what does it matter?
            It's Christmas, I guess it's okay to get fatter."

Dad bit into his doughnut with great affection, savoring each chew of forbidden confection.

He pictured the new cookbook he bought for his bride. He adored the photos of the cookies inside.

Then a thought came to his head and he lost his grin: He hadn't bought it for her; he'd bought it for him.

14

The day, it grew older, and down came the soft snow.
I watched it fall gently from the picture window.

Outside, pine trees slept under a blanket of white.
Although laden with snow, the trees' burdens
    seemed light.

They had all that they needed. They had not a care.
But can a tree parallel the burdens boys bear?

I thought of my *list* and the things I didn't get,
and the corner of my eye began to feel wet.

The cause wasn't the gifts that I didn't receive;
it was something longing on the inside of me.

A tear traveled down my cheek all wet and sloppy,
but I perked up when I saw Grandpa's jalopy.

16

Grandpa lumbered out of his car, slammed the door closed,
and was sprinkled with snow from his head to his toes.

I threw open the door and Grandpa hugged me so tightly;
for he never took the business of hugging me lightly.

His arms held no presents, I didn't understand.
All he brought was an old book held gently in his hand.

We joined at the table beholding our bounty.
Dad makes the best turkey in all of our county.

Upon serving Mom's pie, we had a big chuckle
as Dad sighed and undid his cinching belt buckle.

Our meal was tasty and after we ate,
Grandpa wiped his mouth and pushed back his plate.

He looked out the window and drew in a deep breath,
then let it out slowly 'til he had no air left.

19

"The Christmas we observe in the here and the now,"
Grandpa said, "has come to lose the meaning somehow."

"Fresh pine and sweet oranges—those scents I remember.
They have come to define the month of December.

"Our thoughts are of presents and fancy ways to dine;
but our focus, it seems, has come way out of line.

"The gifts of family and kind simple gestures
have been replaced with lifestyles—wounded and festered."

21

The room, it got quiet,
and we turned a tight ear...

"I remember the Christmas
of my thirteenth year...

"The fire was warm. The decorations were few.
Peace and joy were our presents. Our dinner was stew.

"We felt nothing missing. We were blessed in all things;
for no sorrow is added with gifts from the King.

"My Dad stood next to my chair and hummed a sweet tune.
Then he smiled and pulled out a bright silver spoon.

"He had found it in a trash heap by an old shoe
and knew at once in his heart whom to give it to.

"He tried to hide his smile with a sarcastic pout
and said, 'Son, here's the silver spoon that you were born without.'

We all broke up with laughter, for the world's idea of treasure
had nothing to do with our riches we found in Christ our Savior."

Grandpa's eyes, how they sparkled and to us my Mom remarked,
"Perhaps this is the perfect time to make a brand new start."

23

Grandpa's hand left the table and reached down to his pocket.
He said, "You won't believe it, but that spoon, I still got it."

He placed it on the table right in front of me.
He cleared his throat, sat up straight and said tenderly,

"Do you suppose that Christmas could fit on this shallow utensil?"
I quickly said, "Grandpa, please, the spoon's no longer than a pencil.

"I don't think a rocket ship or our eight-foot Christmas tree
would fit upon the spoon that you have placed in front of me."

Then Grandpa's face, so worn with time,
leaned forward to be nearer mine.

"Yet you cram the Lord Jesus in the smallest corner of your heart,
when in fact He, alone, deserves the very biggest part."

27

28

Grandpa placed his old, worn out book there, upon the table,
and opened it to a page marked with an old soup label.

The room became so quiet we could hear each other breathe.
Grandpa's eyes slowly scanned the page and he began to read.

The Holy Words poured from his lips as he read aloud Luke's Gospel.
I marveled at the miracles ...with God all things are possible.

"Glory to God in the highest!"
heavenly hosts proclaimed.
The truth of Christmas pierced my heart.
Something inside me changed.

Grandpa continued the story then,
"And on earth peace, goodwill toward men."

31

We began to truly walk with God on that awesome
   Christmas day.
The past twenty years, we've found perfect peace in
   doing things His way.

It's true that God chooses foolish things to
   confound the wise.
He used an old man and a spoon to
   open up our eyes.

I can hear the words Grandpa spoke over and over in my head,
as I look out my child's window from the edge of his soft bed.

I thought of how they had no room for Jesus at the inn,
and how that was no different than a heart filled with sin.

The Holy Season means that His love and His Son have made us free.
It is what God has made it and not what we try to make it be.

I treasured this great lesson as I stared up at the moon:

Christmas means what Christmas means,
despite our silver spoons.

35

About The Author

Jennifer Whipple dreamed of being a wife, a mother, and an author—now she is all three.

Photo by Shutterbug Digital of Monroe, MI

Jennifer and her husband Rick live in a quaint bungalow off of a dirt road near the village of Dexter, Michigan. When Jennifer isn't writing, she can often be found playing outside with her two little girls or tending her beautiful flower garden.

Jennifer has been blessed with a wonderful family, friends, neighbors, and a Heavenly Father who loves her very much. While she still dreams of doing many things, she has come to realize that with God, all things are possible…

To order additional copies of **Christmas on a Spoon** or to find out about other books by Jennifer Whipple or Zoë Life Publishing, please visit our website www.zoelifepub.com.

A bulk discount is available when 12 or more books are purchased at one time. For other books for children published by Zoë Life Publishing, contact outreach at Zoë Life Publishing:

Kitty Kate's Tea Party
Written and Illustrated by
Karen Dean

Zoë Life Publishing
P.O. Box 871066
Canton, MI 48187
(877) 841-3400
outreach@zoelifepub.com

**The Wonder of a
Summer Day**
Written by Laura Becker
Illustrated by Jennifer Steffen

**Where Do Crickets Go
when Winter Comes?**
Written by Phyllis Russell-Gilmer
Illustrated by Chamira Jones

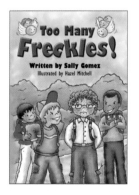

Too Many Freckles
Written by Sally Gomez
Illustrated by Hazel Mitchell

**The Hidden Treasures of
My Kingdom Pals**
Written by Julie Page and
Sabrina Adams
Illustrated by Mike Motz